THIS BOOK BELONGS TO:

_____

Copyright Page:
Big Questions for Little Geniuses: What is AI?
Written, Designed & Illustrated by GiggleTree Publishing
Copyright © 2025 GiggleTree Publishing. All rights reserved.
No part of this book may be reproduced, stored in a retrieval system, or transmitted in any form or by any means, electronic, mechanical, photocopying, recording, or otherwise, without the prior written permission of the publisher, except in the case of brief quotations embodied in critical reviews and certain other noncommercial uses permitted by copyright law.

For permissions or enquiries, please contact:
hello@giggletreepublishing.com
First Edition
ISBN: 978-1-0683541-7-5

Disclaimer:
The content of What Is AI? is intended for educational and informational purposes only and is designed to introduce children aged 6 to 12 to the basic concepts of Artificial Intelligence (AI). While every effort has been made to ensure the information is accurate, simple, and age-appropriate, this book does not aim to provide an exhaustive or technical understanding of AI.
The examples, explanations, and scenarios presented in this book are simplified for young readers and may not fully reflect the complexities or nuances of AI as a field of study or industry practice. Readers are encouraged to explore additional resources and consult professionals or experts for a deeper understanding of AI concepts.
Parents, guardians, and educators are advised to guide children through the book and encourage open discussions about the topics presented. GiggleTree Publishing is not responsible for any misunderstandings or interpretations arising from the content of this book.

Introduction

Welcome to What Is AI?, a fun and exciting journey into the world of Artificial Intelligence. Have you ever wondered how robots can play games, how your favourite apps know what you like, or how computers can recognise faces? This book is here to answer those big questions in a way that's easy to understand and fun to explore.

In this book, we'll take a look at what AI is, how it works, and all the amazing ways it's used in the world today. From teaching computers to learn like humans to imagining what the future might hold, you'll discover the magic behind the machines, and why it's not magic at all, but science!

So grab your curiosity and let's dive into the fascinating world of Artificial Intelligence.

BIG QUESTIONS FOR LITTLE GENIUSES

WHAT IS AI?

A KIDS' GUIDE TO ARTIFICIAL INTELLIGENCE

Table of Contents

① What is AI?..8

② How do machines learn?......................15

③ Is AI around us?..................................23

④ Can machines think like humans?........31

⑤ Can we teach it right from wrong?......38

⑥ How do people build AI?......................46

⑦ What are the coolest AI inventions?...54

⑧ What is the future of AI?.....................60

⑨ What can YOU do with AI?..................66

⑩ Extras: Glossary..................................67

What is AI?

Have you ever wondered how computers can play games, suggest your favourite movies, or even talk to you like a friend? That's all thanks to something called Artificial Intelligence, or AI for short! But what is AI exactly? Let's break it down together.

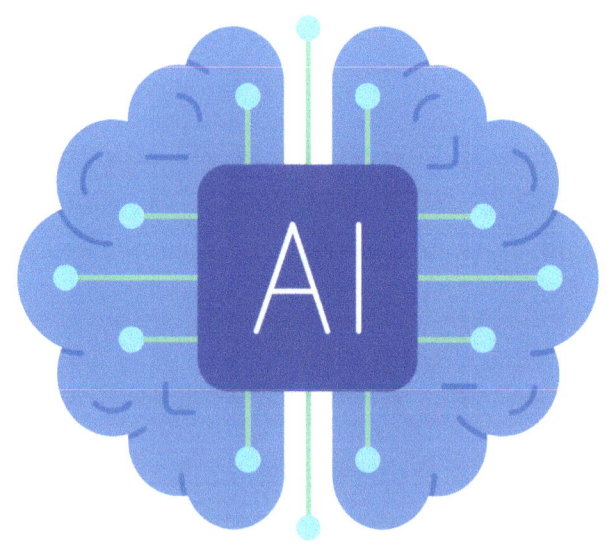

Imagine you have a toy robot. If you press a button, it walks forward. If you press another button, it spins around. That's pretty cool, right? But AI is even cooler. Instead of just doing what it's told, like your toy robot, AI can learn things and make decisions on its own. It's like giving the robot a brain.

AI works by teaching computers how to think and solve problems, kind of like how your teacher helps you learn math or science. Computers don't have real brains like us, but they can use programs to understand patterns and figure things out.

Here's a fun way to think about it: AI is like a magic toolbox. Inside the toolbox are all kinds of cool tools. There's one for recognising faces, another for talking to people, and even one for drawing pictures. The more tools the computer has, the more amazing things it can do. For example, one tool helps your phone understand your voice when you ask it a question, while another tool recommends your favourite songs or movies.

Did you know that AI can also help solve big problems? It's used to predict the weather, find new planets, and even help farmers grow food more efficiently. AI is like a superhero sidekick for humans, helping us do things faster and better. And it's not just about solving problems, AI can also be creative. Have you seen AI-generated art or listened to music made by computers?

One cool thing about AI is how it learns to make decisions. It follows something called an algorithm, which is like a recipe. Just like you might follow a step-by-step recipe to bake cookies, AI follows steps to solve problems and figure things out. The more it practices, the better it gets.

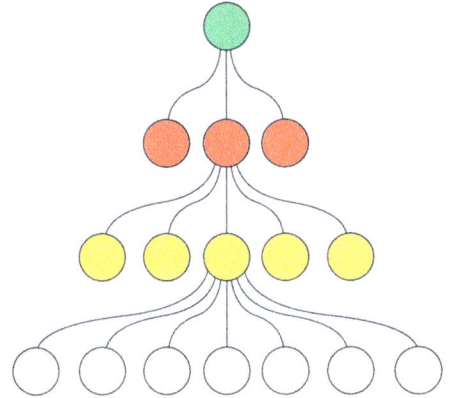

By the end of this book, you'll understand how AI works, why it's so powerful, and how it's changing the world. You might even start dreaming of creating your own AI one day.

AI Spotter Challenge

AI is all around us! With a parent or friend, take a walk around your home or school and write down three things you think might use AI. It could be a voice assistant, a smart TV, or even a game you play. Discuss with someone how each one might use AI and draw a picture of your favourite AI-powered gadget.

How do machines learn?

Learning isn't just for kids like you, computers can learn too. But how do they do it? Let's dive in.

When you learn something new, like how to ride a bike, you practice over and over again until you get it right. Computers learn in a similar way, but instead of practicing, they use data. Data is just a fancy word for information, like pictures, numbers, or words. The more data a computer has, the better it can learn.

Think of a computer like a student and data like a big pile of books. If the student reads all the books, they'll get smarter, right?

Computers "read" data to understand patterns and make decisions. For example, let's say you show a computer 1,000 pictures of cats and dogs. If you tell it which pictures are cats and which are dogs, it can start to tell the difference on its own. That's called machine learning.

But what if the computer makes a mistake? No worries, Just like you learn from your mistakes, computers do too. They use something called "feedback" to get better. For example, if a computer guesses that a dog is a cat, it gets corrected and tries again. Over time, it improves. If they make a mistake, you help them fix it, and they get better with practice.

Some computers use a special kind of learning called deep learning. This is when computers use something called neural networks, which are inspired by how our brains work. It's like giving the computer a tiny brain of its own to help it learn faster and smarter.

Here's a fun example: have you ever wondered how computers can understand your voice? That's another example of machine learning. AI listens to lots and lots of voices, learns the patterns, and figures out what people are saying. So the next time Siri or Alexa gets your question right, you can thank machine learning for that.

Another example is translating languages. AI looks at millions of sentences in different languages to understand how words and phrases match up. Just like having a super-smart dictionary that learns from every sentence it reads.

And did you know that AI can even teach itself by playing games? For example, some AI systems have played thousands of chess games to become champions. They learn from every move and get better each time. Just like when you practice a sport until you are the best player on the field.

Teach the Robot

Pretend you are a computer scientist teaching a robot how to recognise a type of fruit. Choose a fruit (e.g. apples). Make a list of things that describe apples (colour, shape, texture, taste). Now, mix in other fruits, how would you help the robot tell the difference between an apple and an orange?

Congratulations! You've just created a mini 'machine learning' system.

Is AI around us?

Artificial Intelligence isn't just something you read about, it's everywhere around you! From the apps on phones to the games you play, AI is quietly working behind the scenes to make your life easier and more fun. But how does it do all that? Let's take a closer look.

Have you ever noticed how your favourite streaming app seems to know exactly what you want to watch? That's AI at work. It looks at the shows and movies you've already watched and compares them to what other people with similar tastes enjoy. Then, it makes recommendations just for you. Just like a friend who knows all your favourite stories and suggests the best ones to watch next.

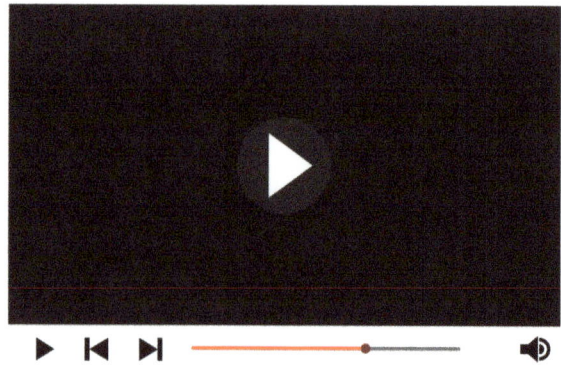

AI also helps when you shop online. Imagine you are looking for a new pair of sneakers. The website might show you options based on your size, favourite colors, and even what other kids your age are buying. AI looks at all this information and says, "Here are the perfect shoes for you". AI can act like your very own personal shopping assistant.

And what about maps? Have you or your parents ever used an app to find the quickest way to school or a friend's house? That's AI too! It looks at traffic patterns, road conditions, and even the time of day to give you the fastest route.

AI doesn't just help with fun stuff, it can also keep you safe. Some cars now have AI systems that can warn drivers about obstacles on the road or even stop the car automatically to prevent an accident. Just like a co-pilot who's always paying attention.

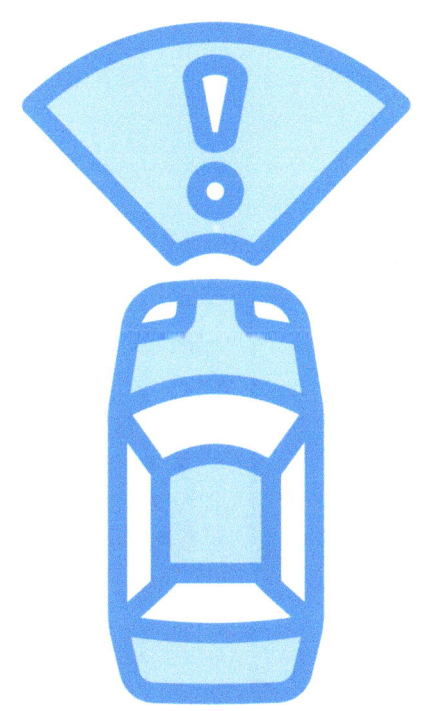

Here's another cool example: voice assistants like Siri or Alexa. When you ask them a question, they don't just magically know the answer. AI listens to your words, figures out what you mean, and searches for the information you need. So when you ask, "How's the weather today?" AI is doing all the behind-the-scenes work to give you the answer.

AI even helps doctors. Imagine a doctor trying to figure out what's making someone sick. AI can look at tons of medical information, way more than a person could and help the doctor find the best treatment. Imagine giving all doctors in the world a superpower to help people faster.

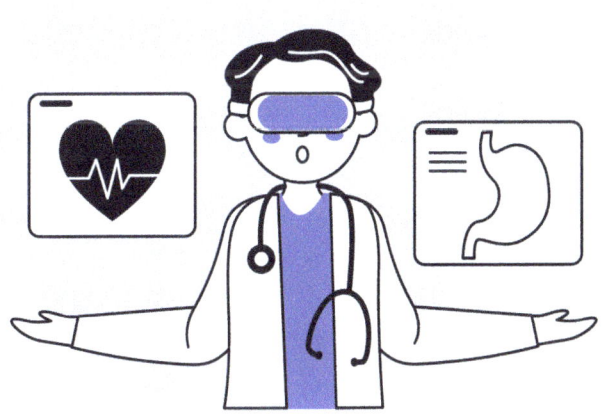

AI Detective

AI is working behind the scenes in many things you use. Think about your favourite apps, websites, or even your school's smartboard. Choose one and research how AI helps it work. For example, if you use YouTube Kids, how does it know which videos you'll like? Create a fun fact card about AI in your chosen app or device!

Can machines think like humans?

When we say "think," we often imagine our own minds, full of ideas, dreams, and questions. But can machines, like computers and robots, think in the same way we do? Let's explore this big question together.

At its core, thinking is about solving problems, making decisions, and coming up with new ideas. AI can solve problems and make decisions, but it doesn't have feelings, dreams, or imagination like humans do. Instead, it uses data and instructions to make choices. For example, a chess-playing AI can think about its next move by calculating all the possible moves on the board. It's super smart at chess, but it doesn't know it's playing a game, it's just following the rules programmed into it.

Some people wonder if AI could ever have emotions or creativity. AI can mimic emotions, like a chatbot that says, "I'm happy to help you!" But it doesn't feel happy, it's just programmed to respond that way. Similarly, AI can create amazing art or music, but it doesn't do it because it's inspired. It's following patterns and instructions it has learned from data.

A famous computer scientist named Alan Turing once came up with a test to see if machines could think. He called it the "Turing Test." If a person talks to a computer and can't tell it's a machine, then the computer might be considered "intelligent." But even if AI passes this test, it's still very different from human thinking.

Here's an example: Imagine you're teaching a robot to bake cookies. The robot can follow the recipe perfectly every time. But if you ask it to invent a new cookie flavor, it might struggle. AI is amazing at following rules and learning patterns, but it doesn't have the spark of creativity that makes humans unique.

Some scientists believe that one day, AI might get closer to human-like thinking. Others think that no matter how smart AI becomes, it will always be different from us. What do you think? Could machines ever truly think and feel like people?

AI vs. Human Brain

Draw two big circles, one for AI and one for the human brain. Write down things AI can do in one circle and things humans can do in the other. In the middle, write things both AI and humans can do. What's different? What's similar? Now, imagine if AI could think exactly like a person, what would be cool, and what might be tricky?

Can we teach AI right from wrong?

AI can do many amazing things, but have you ever wondered how it knows what's the right thing to do? Let's dive into the important topic of teaching AI to make good choices.

Imagine a robot that can help with your homework. Sounds awesome, right? But what if the robot gives you the wrong answers on purpose? That wouldn't be very helpful. To make sure AI does more good than harm, people have to teach it the difference between right and wrong. This is called programming ethics into AI.

For example, when developers create a chatbot to help answer questions, they program it to respond politely and accurately. But if someone tries to trick the chatbot into saying something mean or untrue, it could make mistakes. That's why developers also teach AI to recognise harmful or false information and avoid spreading it.

Another example is self-driving cars. These cars use AI to navigate the roads. But what happens if a car has to decide between stopping suddenly or swerving to avoid an accident? The people who build the car's AI program it to make the safest choice possible. This shows how important it is to think about ethics when creating AI.

But what happens when AI makes mistakes? In 2016, a chatbot was tricked into saying mean things because it was programmed to learn from what people told it. Unfortunately, some users fed it harmful ideas. This is why teaching AI "right from wrong" isn't just about programming it's also about protecting AI from bad influences.

So, how do people decide what's right for AI? They create guidelines to make sure AI is helpful, fair, and safe for everyone. For example, AI used in schools and universities should treat all students equally, no matter where they come from or what language they speak.

AI isn't perfect, and it never will be. But with careful programming and testing, it can become a force for good. The key is for humans to always stay in charge, making sure AI follows the rules we set.

AI Decision Maker

Imagine you are designing a self-driving car. The car comes across a ball rolling into the road. What should it do? What if a child is chasing the ball? Write down the choices the AI car might have and which one you think is the safest. Discuss with a friend or family member how do humans decide what's right and wrong, and can AI learn this?

How do people build AI?

AI might seem magical, but behind every smart machine is a team of hardworking people who build it. Let's uncover the steps they take to create AI.

The first step in building AI is coding. Coding is like writing a set of instructions that tell the computer what to do. Imagine writing a recipe for cookies. You tell the computer, step by step, how to mix the ingredients, shape the cookies, and bake them. In the same way, programmers write "recipes" for AI so it can learn and solve problems.

Next comes collecting data. Remember how AI learns from information, like pictures of cats and dogs? Developers gather tons of data to train the AI. For example, if you're building AI to recognise fruit, you'd collect pictures of apples, bananas, and oranges. The more data AI has, the better it gets at learning.

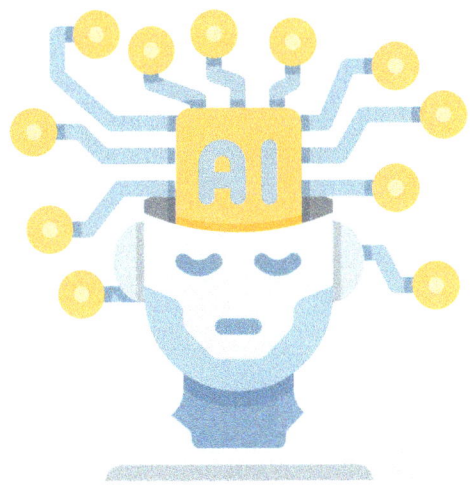

After that, the AI goes through a process called training. This is like practice for the computer. It studies the data and tries to recognise patterns. For example, it might learn that apples are usually red and round, while bananas are yellow and curved. If it makes mistakes, developers fix them and let the AI try again.

But how does AI actually learn? Developers use tools like neural networks, which are inspired by how our brains work. A neural network is a system of "layers" that process information step by step. It's like solving a puzzle, one piece at a time, until the whole picture makes sense.

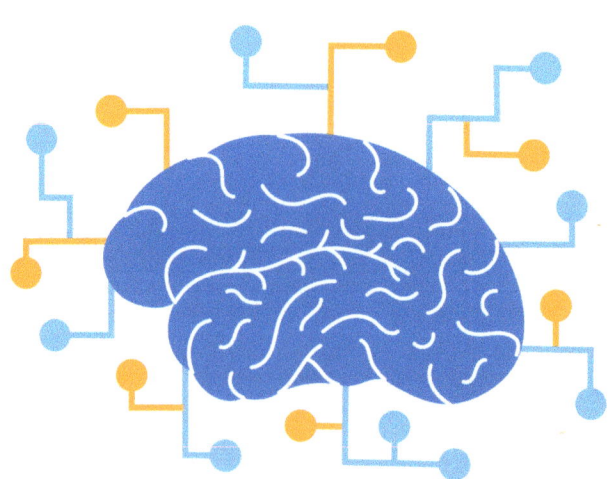

Once the AI is trained, it needs testing. Developers check to see if the AI works correctly. If it's a robot that cleans floors, they test it in different rooms to make sure it can handle carpets, corners, and furniture. If it's a video game character, they test how it reacts to players' actions.

Finally, when the AI is ready, it's launched into the real world. But the work doesn't stop there! Developers keep updating the AI to make it smarter and fix any bugs. This is why your favourite apps and games always have updates, they're getting better thanks to AI improvements.

Code Breaker

AI runs on code. Here's a fun challenge: Write a simple instruction list (algorithm) for how to brush your teeth, but make sure every step is clear (e.g. "Pick up the toothbrush with your dominant hand"). Ask a friend or parent to follow your instructions exactly did they get stuck? That's why AI needs good coding to work properly.

What are the coolest AI inventions?

AI isn't just useful, it's also super cool. Let's explore some of the most amazing AI inventions that are changing the world.

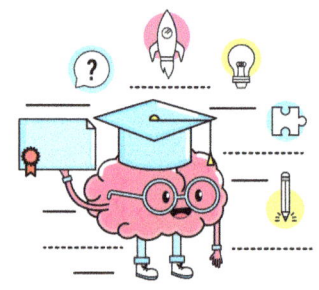

One of the coolest examples of AI is robots. Some robots can walk, talk, and even dance. There are robots that help doctors perform surgeries with precision, robots that explore space, and even robots that help clean up the environment. Imagine a robot that could pick up trash from the ocean that's AI in action!

Another awesome AI invention is self-driving cars. These cars use AI to "see" the road, avoid obstacles, and follow traffic rules. They're like having a super-smart chauffeur who never gets tired. Self-driving cars might even make transportation safer in the future.

Have you ever seen AI create art? Some programs can paint pictures, write stories, or compose music. It's like giving a computer an artist's palette or a composer's piano. For example, there are apps that let you create your own AI-generated artwork with just a few clicks.

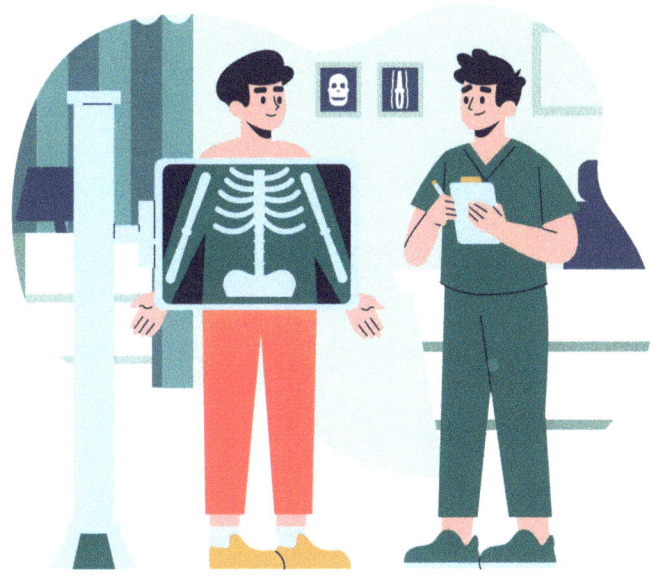

AI is also helping in medicine. There are AI systems that can detect diseases earlier than doctors can. For example, AI can look at X-rays and find tiny signs of illness that might be hard for humans to see. This helps doctors treat patients faster and more effectively.

One of the most fun AI inventions is chatbots. These are programs that can have conversations with you. Some chatbots are so good that it feels like you're talking to a real person. They're used in customer service, online games, and even to help people practice new languages.

AI Invention Challenge

If you could invent an AI machine to help with anything in life, what would it do? Would it help with homework, clean your room, or cook your favourite meal? Draw your AI invention and write a few sentences about what it does and how it learns. Give it a fun name too!

8

What is the future of AI?

What will AI be like in the future? Nobody knows for sure, but one thing is certain: AI will keep getting smarter and more helpful. Imagine schools where AI helps teachers create lessons tailored to each student. If you are great at math but need extra help with reading, AI could design a program just for you. Imagine having a personal tutor in every subject.

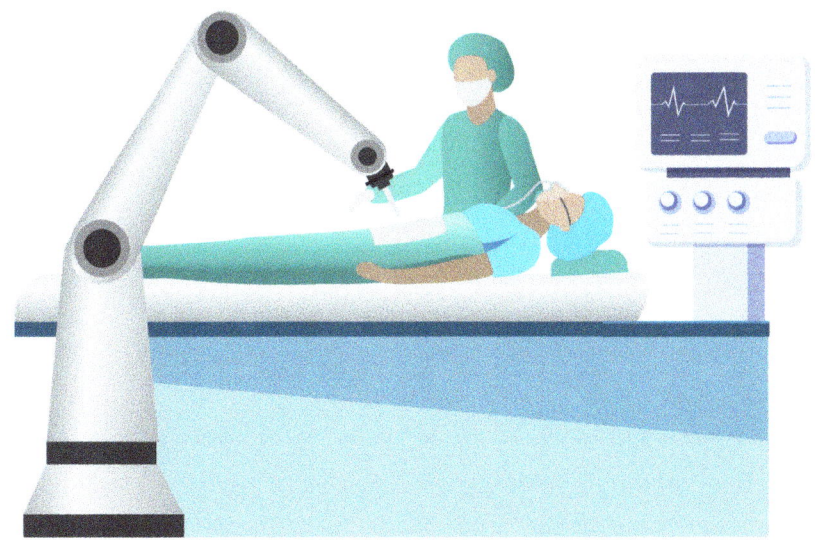

In hospitals, AI might help doctors find cures for diseases faster. It could analyze tons of medical data to discover new treatments and even design medicines. AI might also be used in robotic nurses to assist doctors and take care of patients.

What about space? AI could help astronauts explore planets and moons. Robots with AI could collect samples, study alien environments, and send back information to Earth. Just like having a team of space scientists working around the clock.

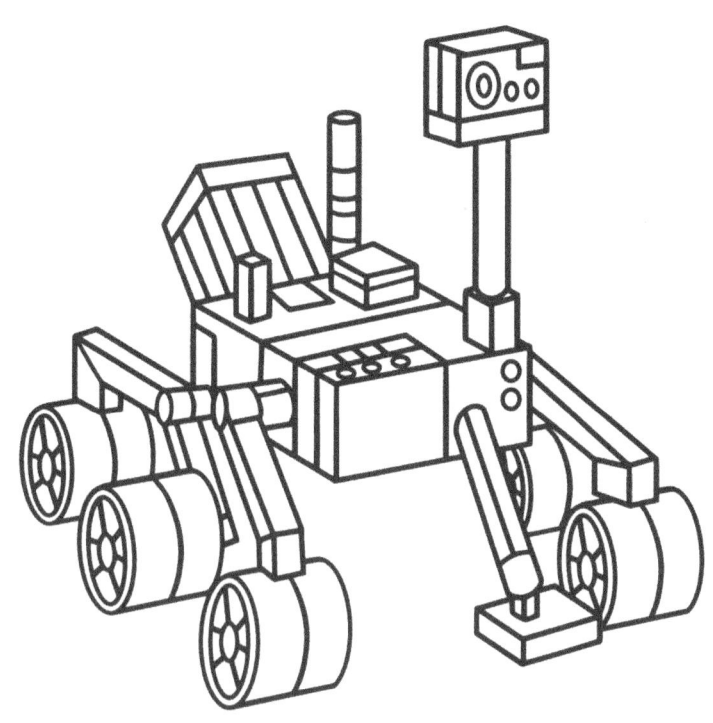

AI could also make everyday life easier. Imagine smart homes where AI controls the lights, temperature, and even cooking. Your house might "learn" your habits and make everything just the way you like it.

But the future of AI isn't just about what it can do, it's also about how we use it. Scientists and engineers are working hard to make sure AI is safe, fair, and beneficial for everyone. That's why it's so important for kids like you to learn about AI. Who knows? You might be the one to create the next big AI invention!

AI Time Machine

Imagine you travel 50 years into the future. What do you see? Are robots delivering food? Are schools taught by AI teachers? Write a short story or draw a comic strip about a future where AI has changed the world. What are the good things? Are there any challenges?

What can YOU do with AI?

AI is all around us, helping us in big and small ways. Now you know what AI is, how it works, and why it's so important. Maybe someday you'll be the one creating the next big AI invention!

With an adult's help, find a beginner coding app and try making a simple project.

Glossary

- **AI (Artificial Intelligence)** - A computer's ability to learn and make decisions like a very smart helper.

- **Algorithm** - A set of instructions or steps, like a recipe, that helps computers solve problems.

- **Data** - Information that computers use to learn, like pictures, numbers, and words.

- **Machine Learning** - A way for computers to get smarter by learning from data and practicing over time.

- **Robot** - A machine that can move, work, or talk, often with the help of AI.

- **Neural Networks** - A computer system that works like a tiny brain, helping it learn and make decisions.

- **Pattern** - Something that repeats or is similar, like stripes on a zebra or a song's rhythm. Computers look for patterns to understand things.

- **Smart Speaker** - A device like Alexa or Siri that uses AI to answer questions, play music, and help you with tasks.

- **Feedback** - Information that helps a computer know if it got something right or wrong so it can improve.

- **Creative AI** - AI that makes art, music, or stories by learning from real artists and musicians.

- **Turing Test** - A test created by a scientist named Alan Turing to see if a computer can act like a human in a conversation.

- **Voice Assistant** - An AI tool that understands your voice and answers questions, like Siri or Google Assistant.

- **Translate** - When AI changes words from one language to another, like from English to Spanish.

- **Traffic Patterns** - The way cars and people move on roads. AI uses this information to help find the fastest route.

- **Recommendation** - A suggestion made by AI, like when it tells you which movie or song you might like.

- **Mistake** - When a computer gets something wrong while learning. AI learns to fix mistakes by practicing.

- **Explorer AI** - AI used to study space, planets, or the ocean to discover new things.

- **Safe AI** - AI that helps keep people safe, like stopping cars from crashing or warning about bad weather.

- **Deep Learning** - A special kind of machine learning where computers use networks inspired by the human brain to solve really hard problems.

- **Recognition** - When a computer can tell what something is, like knowing a picture shows a cat or a dog.

Loved Learning About AI?
Discover other titles in the Big Questions Series
Keep asking Big Questions Little Geniuses!

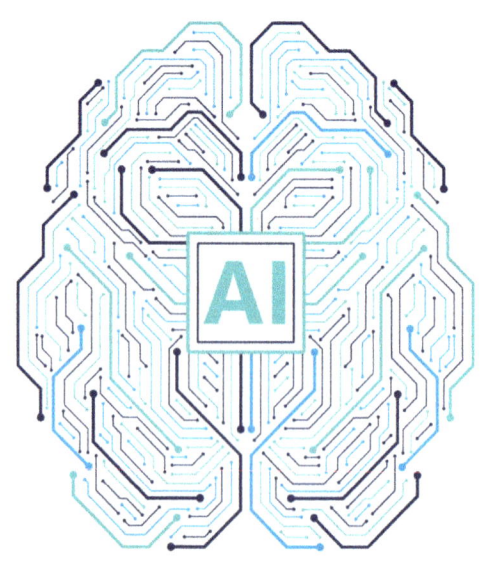

www.ingramcontent.com/pod-product-compliance
Lightning Source LLC
Chambersburg PA
CBHW051603010526
44118CB00023B/2803